HANG ONTO *Your Hats*

A Pictorial Journey of Dorothy Wright Tillman

12-17-08

To Claia Jone

Best Wishe

Dorothy W. T.

DJT Publishing
4645 South King Drive, Chicago, IL 60653
ISBN 978-0-9801721-0-2

First Edition

Written by Dorothy Wright Tillman
Art Direction and Design by Jason A. Nelson
Copy Editing by Ebony Tillman
Additional Copy Editing by Andrea Smith
Cover Photography by Victor Powell
Hat Photography by Jason A. Nelson

Printed by Lammar Offset Printing Limited

A Tribute to My Mother

This book is dedicated in love, respect and gratitude to my mother, Mrs. Edna Mae Wright Struggs. She is a special woman, blessed with an incredible spirit and strength! Her capacity for love is endless. GOD is involved in everything that she does in life, and it is an important lesson she passed down to each of us – put GOD first and he will direct your path. I love her dearly for all she gave and sacrificed to give my brother James Jr., sisters Audrey, Precious, Tammy and me a supporting and loving home. She was a young mother who worked hard for everything we had. She was a domestic who cleaned the homes of whites and cared for their children for $10 a week and never complained, while simultaneously raising her own family as well. She gave us so much love I never knew we were poor. My mother and father, even after they divorced showered us with love, taught us strong principles and moral values and stressed the importance of family. We always have been, and still are to this day - - a warm and close-knit family. I owe everything that I am, and ever will be to her. My mother taught me to love hats and she was my first role model of a lady. Whenever I think of her, I want to give her roses – because I believe that she richly deserves all that is beautiful and wonderful in life. So I say "THANK YOU" mother for everything!

"My mission has never been an easy or a popular one, but it is a mission given to me by GOD, lovingly nurtured by my father, mother, grandmother, along with the men and women of the Civil Rights Movement and the communities I grew up in. I have accepted it with grace and humility, as well as with a deep understanding of the awesome responsibility entrusted in me."

- Dorothy Wright Tillman

Dorothy Tillman is a woman that has never stopped. From Alabama to Chicago, the Edmund Pettus Bridge to the City Council. She has constantly engaged herself on the front line with movements that advanced poor people including fighting for families seeking access to public transportation in California, to several grassroots efforts that led to the election of the legendary politician Harold Washington, Chicago's first Black Mayor. As Alderman of the city's historic and legendary Black south side 3rd Ward for over two decades, she's never still as long as there are social injustices to overcome.

Dorothy Tillman in 1980's

Dorothy Tillman is a multi-faceted jewel with many sparkling prisms, each reflecting a different aspect of her life. As a widely recognized and highly revered woman with a gentle yet vibrant spirit, she is a fighter, a devoted daughter, loving mother and grandmother, visionary, preservationist of Black culture, community builder, civil rights activist and strong woman of God.

Today as she starts a new chapter in a life that has seen her walk with African Kings and world leaders, as well as seniors, mothers with children and everyday people, her vision remains clear: there is so much more to be done in her calling to secure justice, political and social equality as economic opportunity for her people remains the same.

And as with everything she does, she always shines with the radiance of an African Queen when elegantly attired in one of her many hats. Her love of hats of all shapes, colors and designs is a part of her legendary and signature look.

"A hat is a woman's crowning glory. I love the finished look that wearing a hat creates, and the subtle power of its mystique that radiates from the brim of a beautiful, ladylike chapeaux," says Tillman.

According to Ms. Tillman, people often ask, "Why do you always wear hats?" She smiles in the memory. "As a child growing up in the South, we were always around women who wore hats on formal occasions – to church, during funerals and other types of social events. Women were not really considered fully dressed until their hat was added," says Tillman. "It was simply instilled in me at an early age. A lady wears her hat."

Tillman pictured in Montgomery, Alabama with her Aunts Mabel Barker, the matriarch on her father side of the family, and Elsie Witcher, her mother's sister.

Remembering the times she spent at Bell Street Baptist Church in Montgomery, Alabama and Macedonia Baptist Church in Pensacola, Florida, it was the elegantly dressed women wearing hats that she encountered who made a significant impact on her. "These women were constantly seen in public attired in a hat, and it appeared to me that they belonged to a special club where the membership required a hat as a proper head covering. More than anything I wanted to be just like them."

Dorothy Tillman pictured with Jimmy Tillman enjoy a night on the town.

Dorothy Tillman also recognizes that during slavery the enslaved African woman in America continued the tradition of covering her head during worship. This tradition has continued over the years and she has maintained a deep appreciation for the symbolism and meaning that hats have generated in Black women.

But something interesting occurred which solidified her relationship with hats. It was the fight for political empowerment in Chicago. In May 1983, an Aldermanic vacancy opened up in the city's historic south side 3rd Ward, and Mayor Washington appointed Dorothy Wright Tillman as his choice. A political firestorm immediately erupted, and Tillman and her supporters were forced to wage an eleven-month battle to secure her confirmation.

"The Black and progressive communities united behind me in this fight to be seated as Alderman, and they would not give up, no matter what," remembered Tillman. "People from all walks of life were committed and determined to win this fight for dignity, equality and economic opportunity in Chicago. I will be forever respectful and grateful for their support."

This occurred during the legendary "Council Wars", the epic Chicago political battle between Mayor Washington's group of '21' Aldermanic supporters versus the Vrdyolak led '29' faction of Aldermen ', which was designed to stop the Mayor's progressive agenda in the early 1980's, was unprecedented in the city's history, and actively watched by a worldwide audience.

The resistance of the Council to seat her as Mayor Washington's choice as Alderman of the city's 3rd Ward,

sparked massive citywide protests within the Black and Progressive communities, as activists and everyday citizens alike demanded and chanted "Seat Dorothy!"

"Those opposed to Mayor Washington and all that he stood for pulled every political trick in the book, and then some to keep me from becoming Alderman. God, however, had other plans. Man makes assessments but God makes assignments."

"Chicago's 14th Ward Alderman, Edward Burke, had vowed to 'jump out of the window' before ever voting for my confirmation," remembers Tillman. "Opposition leader Alderman "Fast" Eddie Vrdolyak of the 10th Ward on the city's far southeast side, constantly rallied members of the 29 against me and the Mayor, vowing that I would never, ever become confirmed as Alderman of the 3rd ward."

Former 22nd Ward Alderman Frank D. Stemberk, a staunch member of the opposition block '29', had launched a successful court challenge to Mayor Washington's appointment of Tillman using a parliamentary maneuver which asserted that there was no such thing as an "Alderwoman". This challenge was upheld by the courts, forcing Mayor Washington to resubmit her nomination as "Alderman", while the highly contentious and controversial battle waged on to fill the 11 month vacancy.

Mayor Washington said of the opposition, "Those opposed to Dorothy's nomination do so only for negative reasons. They are like Pavlov's dogs. They oppose anything I do by reflex."

During this period of political limbo and the on-going war waged by the '29' to dismantle the programs and policies of Mayor Washington, Black powerhouse businessmen Edward Gardner of Soft Sheen Products, Inc., and legendary publisher John H. Johnson, the founder of Ebony / Jet magazines, were two of Chicago's outstanding leaders who maintained the tradition of activism in the Black community.

Mr. Gardner and Mr. Johnson exemplified the strength and determination of Black leaders who knew what it meant to struggle against politically and racially motivated injustices. They were supportive and called for the confirmation of Dorothy Tillman as Alderman.

Mr. Gardner was among the first Black businessman to support the candidacy of Mayor Harold Washington, and continued that legacy by supporting Tillman as his nominee for the 3rd Ward. He declared that the Third Ward

Confirm Dorothy Tillman

- CHICAGO TRIBUNE, Friday, May 18, 1984

Mulishness is the only reason the city council majority denied confirmation to Dorothy Tillman as alderman of the 3d Ward. Does anyone really believe the aldermen turned her down out of horror at the prospect of sitting near someone who once may have uttered a dirty word?

Mrs. Tillman was rejected by the Rules Committee, headed by Ald. Frank Stemberk (22d), in a 7-4 vote Wednesday. One of the favorable votes was cast by Ald. Fred Roti (1st) of the majority bloc, who said that, whatever his feelings about Mrs. Tillman, the people of the 3d Ward deserve representation. There has been no official alderman since last June when Tyrone Kenner was convicted.

This is one time Ald. Edward Vrdolyak (10th) should chastise his charges. He should call forth his legendary skills at maneuvering and get this matter out of committee and through the council. He would look gracious, proving he really means what he says about reaching accommodation with the mayor. He would be in a position to extract similar accommodation. And he could do it all without damaging the majority bloc's support among its voters, most of whom probably agree with Mr. Roti's assessment.

Mrs. Tillman has the support of the mayor, the minority 20, the 3d Ward constituents, the black community at large and the multi-ethnic Cook County Democratic Women, who stood up for her at the hearing. She was elected ward committeeman with 61 percent of the vote, and will no doubt be a shoo-in next February in the special election to fill the aldermanic vacancy.

The majority bloc has shown many times in the 13-month rule of Harold Washington how meddlesome it can be. This is one fight it shouldn't have picked.

- CHICAGO SUN-TIMES, Friday, May 18, 1984

would have representation and that he would pay her Aldermanic salary and benefits for her family until she was confirmed by the City Council.

Mr. Johnson, knowing Dorothy Tillman since she was a teenager with Dr. Martin Luther King's staff, felt it was "unconscionable" that Tillman's confirmation had been held off so long and pledged to help pay off any incurred campaign debts.

"I'll never forget the tremendous courage and dedication of these two men during this time of extreme challenge and controversy. We knew that I would be confirmed by the Council, and we vowed to keep fighting. These two giants stood with us all the way, and the Black community should never forget that they stood tall on their principles for us all. I personally owe these men a debt of gratitude."

Tillman became known for her hats. She was rarely seen without one. On the day of her inauguration, tensions ran high. The City Council chamber, the gallery and the City Hall hallways were packed with thousands of agitated and screaming supporters, Chicago residents, media reporters and curious onlookers, all with strong feelings, either pro or con, about Dorothy Tillman.

"I was very calm that morning, and prayed with my family before leaving to go downtown to the City Council meeting," remembers Tillman. "I said to myself that God has been in our corner all this time, and I was not going to worry about the outcome – and I knew without a doubt that if it was his will, we would prevail."

One thing was for certain. She chose her hat for that meeting very carefully.

As Tillman entered the City Council Chamber on that important morning, the room was hushed, with all eyes on her.

Tillman leaves another committee hearing where the "29" refused to confirm her.

Walking in the light of supreme confidence that comes from putting the Almighty first in everything that she did, on May 28, 1984, Tillman was escorted to the podium to be sworn in as Alderman by the late great 24th Ward Alderman, William "Bill" Henry, and her political nemesis Alderman "Fast" Edward Vrdolyak.

Tillman was confirmed by a voice vote of the Chicago City Council. As the newly-confirmed Alderman, Tillman took her seat in the council chambers. The City Council Sergeant-at-

Arms, Michael Colletta told her that she could not wear a hat on the Council floor. He ordered her to remove her hat, citing some obscure parliamentary rule. She refused. More confusion ensued, but Tillman would not remove her hat.

A little known aspect to this story however, is the fact that during these controversial times, an older, well-dressed Black woman who, observing these events, took Tillman aside later that day and whispered the words that would shape forever her reputation as "The Hat".

After the council meeting she pulled Dorothy Tillman away from the shouting and chaos in the Council chambers, and told her in a gentle, yet firm manner, "Darling, don't you worry about these people trying to keep you from your God appointed duty, because they will not be victorious, YOU will - - and don't EVER let them see you without your hat!"

Tillman special election victory celebration in 1985 with Mayor Washington.

Needless to say, at the end of that tumultuous day Dorothy Tillman had become the Alderman of the city's Third Ward and a legendary wearer of hats. According to Dorothy Tillman, she never forgot the words of that kind woman. Therefore, from that pivotal day to this one, she is always publicly adorned in one of her countless elegant hats.

Tillman poses en vogue for a special on her hat collection in 1987.

Where does Tillman keep her awesome collection of chapeaux? She has a special area in her turn-of-the-century home where she puts them in carefully labeled boxes. So many people from throughout the United States and the world have presented her with hats for special occasions as gifts and tokens of appreciation, that she feels truly blessed to have gathered such a collection.

"I love all my hats, especially those given to me by others. It shows they've taken the time to do something to say 'thanks' or because they want to make you happy," says Tillman. While she has never counted them all, she guesses that they must literally be several hundreds of hats in her collection.

Tillman's hats span the spectrum and tell an amazing story of a life of service and activism - - there are working hats and caps, hats she wears just for fun, every-day business and professional hats, hats for churches, funerals and other major events. There are hats she wears when invited to speak at civil rights rallies, mass meetings and political forums. There are hats she wears for social occasions and that knock-out, drop dead glamorous hats for those times when nothing but the height of sophisticated elegance and style will do.

Everyone wants to know where she gets her hats. Besides those she has received as gifts, many of Tillman's hats originated from a small neighborhood clothing store run by a woman known as 'Eloise'. A long-time Grand Boulevard / Bronzeville business owner, the late Eloise was well-known and widely respected for her business ability, and for her superb sense of style. Her shop was located on 47th Street, and was 'the' place for one-of-a-kind hats worn by well-dressed women throughout the decades. She provided hats to everyone - - the stars of the era – including Dinah Washington, to the 'first ladies' of churches, business women as well as ladies of leisure. According to Tillman, she and Eloise have been profiled together in many television programs, magazine and newspaper articles.

Ms. Eloise and Alderman at her shop on 47th St.

"I purchased my hats at Eloise's because of the quality and selection she carried in her store. It was also a local neighborhood Black business that deserved our support. Her selections

Tillman stand in front of her 1st campaign poster dressed in traditional African wear.

rivaled anything that existed in other areas of the city, I loved going in there to see what was new and exciting," said Tillman.

"Women all over the world wear hats. It is especially important to recognize that wearing head covering is an ancient African tradition that continues to exist today. When I traveled to Ghana and other countries in Africa, I witnessed the beauty and dignity of the women who splendidly wrapped their heads as they went out in public. Entire families take pride in being well-dressed- - and this is a tradition we must continue," emphasizes Tillman.

"Finally, as women, we must raise our young girls to accept their feminine grace, and not be afraid to dress and look their best. We are queens! The wearing of hats is a natural part of our history, and future generations of Black girls and young women must be taught to embrace their responsibility to carry on this time-honored tradition of grace and elegance."

"We must hang onto our hats!"

HANG ONTO *Your Hats*

A Pictorial Journey of Dorothy Wright Tillman

Tillman enjoys a moment with her younger sister Audrey Faye Slaughter, of Pensacola, Florida and co-host Bobby "Blue" Bland backstage at the Roots Festival (Our mother loves Bobby).

Tillman greeting and enjoying her guests at the 15th annual "Bring it on Home to Me" Roots Festival reception, with co-host Millie Jackson in background.

Tillman sings a song with Vance Kelly and Ms. Lee owner of the famous Chicago club Lee's Unleaded Blues, one of the sponsors of the annual "Bring It on Home to Me" Roots Festival.

Alderman Tillman joins Mayor Washington at the podium in City Council to salute 3rd and 4th ward visitors. Former Alderman Timothy Evans is on the right.

Alderman Tillman and 22 year community staff representative Qwin Dixon, who grew up in the Robert Taylor Homes. He played a very pivotal role in organizing young men in the section called "The Hole" to join him to elect Chicago's first Black mayor.

Tillman with the late Congressman Charles Hayes, 1st District, Illinois and the late Cardiss Collins, Congresswoman of the 7th District, Illinois.

Long time friend, Former Illinois State Representative Monica Faith Stewart (L), the late Mayor Harold Washington, unidentified supporter and Alderman Tillman taking a stroll down memory lane.

Tillman is attired for an elegant afternoon soiree, with a chic brown leopard wide brim hat, complete with ribbons, feathers and rhinestones. She poses with Melody Spann-Cooper, President and CEO of the historic Black-owned Chicago WVON radio station, 1690-AM at the Harold Washington Cultural Center reception for the 2007 Black United Fund of Illinois "Passing the Torch – Living Legends" Awards.

Tillman has a love for cowboy hats and cowboy boots. She poses with members of the Broken Arrow Riding Club during their annual High Noon Ride in Washington Park, in Chicago. She is very supportive of the Black Cowboys and Cowgirls. She considers herself an honorary member.

Tillman and Jamaican Consul General Lloyd Hyde and his wife Peach at the Caribbean Festival, where she was one of the judges for the festivities.

Alderman Tillman greets the world-renowned Grammy®-award winning songwriter and performer the late, great Pop Staples, father of the famous, Chicago-based Staple Singers at the "Bring it on Home to Me" Roots Festival.

Radiant in creamy white, Tillman is saluted during Black History Month, for "A Lifetime of Struggle" at the DuSable Museum of African American History in Chicago. She is addressing the audience as her daughter Ebony stands near an award winning photo of Tillman being arrested by police in San Francisco.

The Honorable James "Jim" Houlihan, Cook County Assessor (Center) congratulates the Honorable Alderman Dorothy Tillman at the DuSable Museum of African American History.

The Honorable Jaques Baudin, Attorney General of the Government of Senegal, discusses plans for the African Village retail and cultural arts complex with Alderman Dorothy Tillman. Baudin also serves as the Mayor of the City of Diourbel.

Fit for a Queen! Alderman Tillman's soaring geometric black-and-ivory hat includes a beautifully intricate pattern of sequins, pearls and beading, as she joins radio personality Tom "The Fly Jock" Joyner and Rev. Willie Taplin Barrow, also known as 'the Little Warrior', co-founder emeritus of the Rainbow PUSH Coalition.

Alderman Tillman is presented a time capsule from Commissioner John Markowski (2nd - left), Illinois State Senator Donnie Trotter, during the grand re-opening ceremonies of the Wabash YMCA at 38th & Wabash in Chicago, former Assistant Housing Commissioner Andrea Smith (left). The historic Wabash YMCA was the birthplace of Negro History Week.

The images of ice crystal, satin, white roses and crisp linen are   an interesting counterpoint to the serious work undertaken by Alderman Tillman, who poses with Martin King, III, following the reception honoring the street-naming ceremony for his father Dr. Martin Luther King, Jr. in Pensacola, Florida.

Alderman Tillman addresses students and staff at Chicago State University during Black History Month, speaking on reparations for the descendants of enslaved Africans in America.

Tillman poses with former U.S. Ambassador and Mayor of Atlanta, Georgia, the Honorable Andrew Young and Tobacco Road Inc. board member H. Lorraine Jeter, past Worthy Grand Matron of Eureka Grand Chapter, OES, State of Illinois PHA.

Alderman Tillman in yellow suit at Chicago City Council chambers during one of her inauguration ceremonies.

A southern belle launches into direct action in support of the use of herbal medicines, and to stop the jailing and harassment of those who provided it, at a rally in front of the Federal Building in downtown Chicago. She was invited by the world renowned late Dr. Alvenia Fulton, a pioneer of holistic medicines.

Tillman gives a passionate speech to a meeting of the Cook County Democratic Women about the importance of women being elected to public office and the natural instinct of women to nurture our children and poor people.

GRAND BOULEVARD PLAZA
A HAROLD WASHINGTON LEGACY
HIS PASSION, LOVE AND COMMITMENT TO THE
PEOPLE OF THE THIRD WARD, HIS HOME,
AND HIS DEDICATION TO NEIGHBORHOOD
REVITALIZATION WAS THE INSPIRATION FOR

GRAND BOULEVARD PLAZA

THIS IS THE REALITY OF
CHICAGO WORKING TOGETHER.

DEDICATED
THIS NINTH DAY OF APRIL 1989
TO THE MEMORY OF
MAYOR HAROLD WASHINGTON
APRIL 15, 1922 – NOVEMBER 25, 1987

A. Mayor Washington and Alderman Tillman smile while holding a rendering of the Grand Boulevard Plaza, one of the community's first Tax Increment Finance and the last economic development project that Mayor Washington broke ground for in October 1987. Alderman Tillman and John Veasley, the first supervisor of maintenance at the Grand Boulevard Plaza, stands in front of the plaque that was dedicated to the memory of Mayor Washington.

The Honorable Rod Blagojevich, Governor of Illinois, addresses one of Alderman Tillman's weekly community meetings.

Spending quality time with her family is an equally precious endeavor for Tillman, who is seen here with her two of her daughters: (Left) Jimalita and Gimel. She dresses well for all of the important people in her life and her hat is part of the fashionable equation.

Alderman Tillman meets with distinguished minister Dr. I.V. Hilliard, Pastor of the New Light Christian Church Center in Houston Texas, who was the special guest of Pastor Richard D. Holmes, Jr. and member of the Morning View "Word" Church in Chicago. L-R: Minister Lydecia Holmes, Pastor Richard D. Holmes, Sr., Alderman Tillman, Dr. Bridgett Hilliard and Dr. I.V. Hilliard.

Tillman joins former Police Superintendent Terry Hilliard honoring fallen Chicago Police officers with the Gold Star memory lane.

Tillman is joined by members of the R&B group Harold Melvin's Blue Notes at the Roots Festival.

Tillman greets the late Blues legend Tyrone Davis (Right) and James Leatherwood (Left) backstage at Roots Festival.

Tillman greets Blues artists Otis Clay (Center), who serves as President of the Board of Directors for Tobacco Road, Inc. and her aunt Mrs. Louise Harris, from Detroit, Michigan.

Tillman, Bobby "Blue" Bland and the late great Little Milton.

A meeting of the hats and minds. Alderman Tillman joins Mrs. Janie Bennett, Chicago businesswoman, long-time friend and supporter and member of the Board of Tobacco Road, Inc (TRI).

Tillman stands with her 'political mentor and mother' Jacky Grimshaw, who served as Mayor Washington's Director of Intergovernmental Affairs (Left) and the Rev. Al Sampson, Pastor of Chicago's Fernwood United Methodist Church. Rev. Sampson was ordained as a minister by Dr. King.

Tillman and Mayor Washington at his birthday celebration. Happy birthday Harold.

Tillman and Dr. Conrad Worrill (R), currently Director of the Jacob H. Carruthers Center for Inner City Studies at Northeastern Illinois University in Chicago, in the early days following a broadcast at the legendary WVON Radio in Chicago.

Alderman Tillman conferring with Reverend C.T. Vivian as Rev. B. Herbert Martin looks on.

Alderman Tillman strolling in downtown Chicago with Fred Rice, former Chicago Superintendent of Police, appointed by Mayor Washington as the 1st African American superintendent.

The late Mayor Washington and Tillman look on at No Crime Day, in Chicago's Washington Park, sponsored by Ed Gardner's Soft Sheen.

A close-up of Alderman Tillman in a ladylike hat and outfit in stunning shades of lavender.

Tillman joins her colleagues at the Chicago City Council during her swearing-in ceremonies 2003.

Tillman and her children smile for the camera following her City Council 2003 inauguration. From Left: Bemaji, Jimalita, Ebony, Alderman Tillman, Gimel and Jimmy,II.

Tillman escorts Mrs. Mamie Till-Mobley, past the plaque that stated the building was built in 1846-47 by slave labor, and hand made bricks, leading to the Jackson, Mississippi City Hall for a hearing. The state of Mississippi apologized to Mrs. Mobley for the brutal slaying of her son Emmett in 1955.

"I never thought I would never set foot in Mississippi again. God knows I feel as if a great weight has been lifted from my heart," said the late Mrs. Mobley following the emotional hearing.

Jackson, Mississippi Councilman Kenneth Stokes, of the 3rd Ward, who spearheaded the event, invited Tillman, of Chicago's historic 3rd Ward, to attend the reparations hearing and apology with Mrs. Till-Mobley.

Tillman, Mrs. Janie Bennett (2nd – Left), family members and well-wishers celebrate the 102nd birthday of Mrs. Olivia White.

Tillman addresses audience at PUSH during the Smithsonian Institute's National Museum of American History presentation of Liberalism on Trial: The African American Freedom Struggle in the Midwest, 1940-1966.

Tillman speaks at a citywide support rally, held at Chicago's historic Tabernacle Missionary Baptist Church. The rally was held after she was sued for removing an inappropriate painting of the late Mayor Washington dressed in lady's underwear, hanging in the Art Institute of Chicago.

Artists have always supported Tillman. Here she shares a moment of laughter with musician and arranger Willie Henderson, (Center) who organized Black Artists for Tillman (BAT).

The crowds tell the story at the Roots Festival – a free annual event which drew over 300,000 attendees annually to the corner of 47th and King Drive in Chicago.

Chicago Police Sergeant Elvin Boone,(L) Radio personality LaDonna Tittle, Tillman and Bob Hill owner of WNRE 980 AM, Pensacola, northern Florida's largest Black own station.

Dorothy Tillman and Clarence Carter laugh about times in Montgomery, Alabama as he prepares to take the stage.

A. Tillman leads a group of parents, as head of the Parent Equalizers, who were committed to balancing the scale of education for our children. Seen here with the 'Bogan Broads', who fought to keep Black children out of Chicago's southwest side schools.

An angry confrontation erupts between Tillman and a member of the Chicago Police department, assigned to protect the Bogan Broads during the school board meeting.

The A-Team. Tillman and the 3rd Ward original aldermanic and state representative staff. Standing, Left to Right: Qwin Dixon, Adrienne Jones, the late Matilda Jefferson, Lovie Copeland, and Frank Garrett. Seated, front row, L-R: Ken Jackson, Alderman Tillman, and former State Representative Paul Williams. Not pictured Doretha Flemmings.

Reverend Jesse L. Jackson, Sr. and Tillman at a reception. Both worked on Dr. Martin Luther King, Jr. staff.

Minister Louis Farrakhan, head of the Nation of Islam (NOI) and Alderman Tillman, wearing a stunning, yet serious silver and black creation, at the program commemorating 10th Anniversary of the Million Man March, held on October 16, 2005 at the Harold Washington Cultural Center in Chicago. Tillman was an original member of the 1995 Million Man March Organizing Committee. She organized several bus-loads of men from Chicago who attended the march and has worked closely with the Minister and the Nation over the years. Below is a bus boarding pass from the original Million Man March. BBC rode one of the buses and documented her sons Jimmy, II and Bemaji, along with their father Jimmy I.

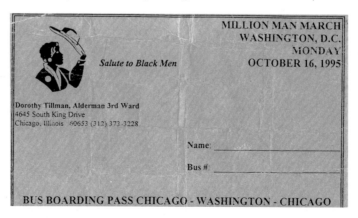

Tillman kneels in honor at the gravesite of President Nkrumah in Ghana.

Tillman greets fellow admirers at the gravesite and home of the legendary Black liberationist W.E.B. Du Bois in Accra, Ghana.

A Journey to the Motherland. Tillman, wearing a green straw hat, places a floral reef at the Kwame Nkrumah mausoleum and memorial park, the final resting place of the first President of Ghana, Africa. It was here that Nkrumah gave his fiery speech proclaiming Ghana's independence.

Tillman wears a close-fitting burgundy velvet cloche adorned with a rhinestone brooch at Rev. Horace Smith's street naming ceremony.

Attorney Paul Williams and his "Political Mother" Dorothy Tillman.

Portrait of Power: Cook County Recorder of Deeds Eugene Moore and Alderman Tillman share a moment of laughter.

Businessman, developer, and long time friend and supporter, Elzie Higginbottom (Left), Tillman and Munir Muhammad, president of the Coalition for the Remembrance of Elijah Muhammad (CROE) and host of the cable TV show "Muhammad and Friends".

Alderman Tillman with supporter and family friend Mr. Russell Vanoy, who worked very hard to insure that she became elected, a founding member of CBUC and BIPO, and retired school teacher.

Hayelom Ayele, former African Affairs director at the Department of Human Relations for the City of Chicago meets with Alderman Tillman.

Tillman and the late A. Patterson Jackson, pastor of Chicago's Liberty Baptist Church, a beacon for the liberation of Black people. Liberty was one of the first Black churches to open its doors to Dr. King on his sojourn to Chicago.

Tillman, Ebony magazine executive editor and historian Lerone Bennett, Jr. (Center), the late Johnson Publishing CEO John H. Johnson (3rd from right) welcomes the late Honorable Cheikh Mourtadha MBacke, leader of the Sufi Muslim Order, in Senegal, West Africa, and an African delegation visiting the Downtown Chicago headquarters of the Johnson Publishing Company.

Alderman Tillman, Mayor Washington and long time friend and supporter Daniel Rozier, at a reception.

Esther Rolle, the actress who played 'Florida Evans' on the television show enjoying "Good Times" with Tillman at a rally to re-elect Mayor Washington.

Tillman and entertainer Redd Foxx, who attended DuSable High School with the late Mayor Washington, visits the 3rd ward.

Mayor Washington speaks at Rev. Louis Rawls 43rd anniversary celebration with Tillman and the late Illinois State Senator Richard Newhouse (Far Right).

The Honorable Mamadou Diop, former Mayor of Dakar, Senegal, speaks at podium during National Summit on Africa in Chicago, while Tillman and Mayor Daley look on.

Don Richards, a Chicago advertising executive discusses issues with Tillman at a Congressional fundraiser at the Haymarket House in Chicago, Illinois.

As proud as a peacock. Tillman and legendary entertainer and native Chicagoan, the late Lou Rawls, founding member of Tobacco Road, Inc. (2nd-Left), join late Illinois State Representative Lou Jones (Left) and late Senator Margaret Smith (2nd-Right) at Tillman's reception for her campaign for the 7th Congressional district seat. Tillman came in a close second among a field of ten candidates.

A meeting of historic civil rights greats: Fred Shuttlesworth (left), Martin King, III, (2nd from right) Tillman and Ben Chavis (far right) at the annual jubilee commemoration of "Bloody Sunday", crossing the Edmund Pettus bridge.

Thousands of marchers join in crossing the Edmund Pettus Bridge.

Tillman, a native of Montgomery, shares a moment with Mrs. Johnnie Carr, one of her Civil Rights mothers, a founding member of the Montgomery Improvement Association (MIA).

Tillman speaks at a youth rally following the Edmund Pettus bridge anniversary commemoration.

Alderman Tillman presenting the late State Representative Lou Jones with a replica of the Harold Washington Cultural Center. Rep. Jones secured state funding for the construction of the center.

Tillman at the Harold Washington Cultural Center in a black-and-white ensemble with matching hat.

Floral splendor. Tillman stands by a striking mosaic of the Late Mayor Harold Wash-ington. Tillman wears a ladylike straw and floral creation, highlighted by a peach rose.

Comedian Bill Cosby tours 47th street with Tillman to support the construction of the cultural center and African American culture.

Internationally-recognized sculptor Ed Dwight, Tillman and famed bluesman Buddy Guy share a moment on the corner of 47th Street and King Drive.

Soft Sheen Products, Inc. founder Edward Gardner and Tillman at "No Crime Day", sponsored by Black-on-Black Love, Inc., a nonprofit, organization established by Gardner.

Dignitaries enjoyed the dedication of the Robert Taylor family playground. L-R: Joseph Shuldiner former head of CHA, Juwan Howard of the Washington Wizards, Alderman Tillman, Ron Carter, CHA and Mildred Dennis, Local Advisory Council (LAC) president.

A victorious Dorothy Tillman, wearing a stunning blue and sequin creation, is surrounded by well-wishers and supporters, savors an election victory in her 3rd ward office, with the ever watchful eyes of the Chicago media recording the moment.

Alderman Tillman joins the Sengstacke and Abbott families at the street naming and dedication ceremony for Robert S. Abbott, the founder of the legendary Chicago Defender newspaper.

Jennifer Iwuchuku, resident and one of the community leaders with Alderman Tillman in her community service office.

Tillman stands with her long-time attorney, Tom Johnson, who has been a stalwart in the liberation struggle for all people.

CITIZEN
CHATHAM-SOUTHEAST
CHICAGO, IL.
Week of October 12, 2005

Audit Bureau of Circulations Member

Celebrating 40 Years of Service to You!

Tillman's delegation assess Hurricane Katrina damage in Mississippi

Group meets with locals to discuss rebuilding plans
by Lesley R. Chinn

MISSISSIPPI—Flipped cars, ripped business signs, twisted railroad tracks, uprooted trees, and caved-in roofs—was a disturbing sight to see for anyone witnessing Hurricane Katrina wrath for the first time.

This is what Ald. Dorothy Tillman (3rd) and a Chicago delegation saw during a fact-finding trip last week to Gulfport and Waveland, MS. Their goal: to help Black residents rebuild a viable community.

"We came down to help, not take over," Tillman stated. "We know how to save communities and know how to rebuild them. We can rebuild Mississippi in a couple of years, but it is going to take a lot."

The trip began with a stop first in

continued on page two

Ald. Dorothy Tillman (3) and William Garth, publisher of the Citizen Newspapers greet Jackson Advocate publisher Charles Tisdale. Photo by:

Newspaper article in the Chicago Citizen newspaper featuring Tillman with two giants in the Black newspaper publishing business, William Garth (Left), owner of the Citizen Newspaper chain and the late Charles Tisdale, staunch civil rights activist and renowned publisher of the Jackson, Mississippi Advocate.

Tillman, wearing a hat of spring green and white denoting renewal and hope, joins a group of dedicated volunteers, including the Seniors of the 3rd Ward, to prepare boxes of donated supplies. This is one of many humanitarian and disaster relief drives Tillman organized as Alderman for those in need following Hurricane Ivan, which hit Pensacola, Florida and other natural disasters.

Tillman stands at the shore in Gulfport, Mississippi, where a whole community had been flatten by Hurricane Katrina. She is examining the only thing that was left standing.

Tillman presents a check to NEIGHBORS in Jackson, Mississippi, an organization who found housing for displaced Hurricane Katrina victims.

Tillman, invited to attend a community rally by Mr. and Mrs. Tisdale of the Jackson Advocate, stands with Hurricane Katrina survivors, elected officials, and rally organizers.

Alderman Tillman greets the late actor Carl Wright, friend and long time Chicago comedian, who appeared in Soul Food as well as other movies and television productions.

Tillman and Queen of the Blues, Koko Taylor , pitches a "Wang Dang Doodle" to celebrate Taylor's birthday.

Tillman, along with Legendary radio hall of fame inductee, and the 'Mayor of Bronzeville' Herb 'The Cool Gent' Kent, who emceed the Roots Festival for fifteen years, joins fellow Chicago WVAZ (V-103) radio personalities Ramonski Luv, the late Ray "Tornado" Little (waving) backstage at Roots Festival.

The stars are shining on Tillman's radiant red outfit and matching hat as she and Tobacco Road, Inc. board member Terry Bell, a local businessman greets the incomparable and sultry soul singer Millie Jackson (center).

Dorothy Tillman joins Mrs. Goodloe on a stroll down the runway at Houston's God's Grace Community Church Scholarship Fundraiser, where Tillman modeled in a fashion show.

Tillman proudly stands with Addie Wyatt and Willie T. Barrow at a campaign stop to re-elect Harold Washington, mayor for the City of Chicago.

The late Lutrell "Lu" Palmer, a hard-hitting and widely respected Black journalist and community activist, and founder of CBUC and BIPO. Palmer, who played a major role in the election of Chicago's first Black Mayor Harold Washington, stands with Tillman at campaign headquarters.

Tillman's children are no strangers to Mayor Washington, who they considered their surrogate grandfather, enjoy an after school surprise visit to the Robert Taylor Boys and Girls club with mom and the mayor. Gimel (2nd, Left) and Jimalita Tillman (Center), who became the Executive Director of the Harold Washington Cultural Center.

The two Dorothy's of Chicago politics embody elegance and sophistication. Alderman Dorothy Tillman and Clerk of the Circuit Court Dorothy Brown are dressed to impress in their black and gold sequin encrusted evening hats.

Alderman Tillman's close profile in a stellar Black and Gold hat embossed in gold nailhead trim. Tillman was speaking at a reparations conference in Minnesota.

Tillman, chairman and founder of the National Reparations Convention Committee, invited to have dinner in the home of a Minnesota family, with co-chair Veronica Burt (R) and regional coordinators Robin Brown and Callie Flournoy-Riser (L) after dinner in their home.

Delores Woods, the Late Mayor Washington's personal secretary and Alderman Tillman share a light moment after a City Council ceremony.

During a ceremony honoring the late Mayor Washington at City Hall, Tillman greets Mayor Washington's family. His brother, Ramon Price (3rd from Left) and his sisters are joined by Alderman William Shaw.

Tillman gives a passionate speech in a packed City Council chamber during the recognition ceremony for the late Mayor Harold Washington.

ALDERMAN DOROTHY TILLMAN JOINS RIOT SURVIVORS AS THEY FILE IN THE HIGHEST COURT

Alderman Dorothy Tillman,3, joined survivors of the 1921 Tulsa Race Riot – some over 100 years old- as they visited the U.S. Supreme Court on Wednesday, March 9th, seeking justice and reparations from the City of Tulsa and the State of Oklahoma. The Tulsa Race Riot is one of our nation's worst incidents of racial violence.

African-American survivors of the "Riot" filed a lawsuit against the City and State after an official Commission established by the State of Oklahoma determined that government officials had not, as authorities had led the public to believe, been overwhelmed by white vigilantes, but had actively organized and participated in mob violence that overnight killed over 300 African-Americans, burned 42 square blocks to ashes, and left 8,000 Greenwood residents homeless and penniless. Plaintiffs are

Harvard Professor Charles Ogletree and Alderman Dorothy Tillman on the steps of the US Supreme Court in Washington, DC.

seeking restitution and repair of the injuries caused by the City and State. The plaintiffs include noted historian Dr. John Hope Franklin, who served as the Chair of President Clinton's Commission on Race and whose father's law office was burned to the ground by rioters.

"There has been a conspiracy of silence about the Black holocaust for much too long. My people are still struggling under the economic, social and psychological effects of slavery today (Post Traumatic Slavery Syndrome). I am honored to join these courageous elders in Washington," said Alderman Tillman.

"It's time America stop denying its ugly past, and what was done to Black people. This nation has never recognized our sacrifices and contributions. We not only built the country with free labor, but despite years of hatred, brutality and legal

Please turn to page 7

Tillman wore a strong red hat, trimmed in black, reminiscent of the color of the blood shed during the summer of 1921, as she fought to honor the survivors of the Tulsa, Oklahoma Race Riots all the way to the U.S. Supreme Court. Here she stands with the living survivors and the group's attorney, Dr. Charles Ogletree of Harvard Law School. Standing, L-R: Tillman, Detroit Councilwoman Joann Watson, Harvard Professor Charles Ogletree. Seated Otis Clark, Eddie Faye Gates, and Wess Young.

Tillman is photographed during the WVON "Friends for a Cure", Breast cancer awareness program, in honor of the late Carolyn Adams, the director of the Illinois Lottery at the Harold Washington Cultural center. Over 1,000 people attended the event. Tillman pushed relentlessly for the center, named in honor of the late Mayor Harold Washington, who honed his political skills in the historic 3rd ward where the center is located.

WGN-TV Anchor Steve Saunders laughs with Tillman and Cirilo McSween, a businessman and disciple of Dr. Martin Luther King, Jr. during an interview at the Chicago-based studio. Tillman jokes "McSween always followed the money. When we went to jail he would find the funds to bail us out of jail."

Tillman, Saunders and McSween following the interview. Tillman and Mr. McSween (right) worked with Dr. King and SCLC.

WLS cameraman Ken Bedford, Chicago public radio host Richard Steele, singer Denise LaSalle, Alderman Dorothy Tillman, V.P of communication for Clear Channel Angela Ingram, and WVAZ (V103 FM) radio personality Herb Kent.

Tillman chats with businessman E.K. Lewis at the 23rd annual 3rd Ward Family Affair Thanksgiving Dinner at the Dawson Technical Center.

After delivering a spiritual Women Day speech at the Fern-wood Methodist Church in Chicago, Tillman is presented a sacred African Cloth by its pastor Rev. Albert Sampson.

Wrapped in traditional African garb, Tillman confers with Dr. Dorothy I. Height, civil rights pioneer and head of the National Council of Negro Women.

Tillman and three of her five children: Jimmy,II (Left), Ebony (2nd, Right) and Bemaji (Right).

The DuSable High School Sanctuary was developed to create an eco-system within the school. It allows biology students to study how plants and animals interact with each other and toward each other. Alderman Tillman, who helped to secure funding to restore the sanctuary and is joined by State Rep. Ken Dunkin (2nd left), principal Carol Briggs, (center) internationally known scientist and retired DuSable teacher Dr. Emiel Hamberlin (far right).

Alderman Tillman introduces U.S. Senator and Presidential candidate, the Honorable Barack Obama, to the enthusiastic crowd at the "Bring it on Home to Me" Roots Festival.

Former U.S. Senator from Illinois, and Ambassador Carol Moseley Braun and Tillman during a meeting. Braun was the first woman and Black elected U.S. senator from Illinois.

Tillman joins former South African President Nelson Mandela at a reception during his visit to Chicago.

Alderman Tillman, Former South African president Nelson Mandela, and Alvin Boutte, Sr. on stage in Chicago after Mandela's release from prison.

Tillman reflects as she stands on the Cape Coast of Ghana, on top of the oldest and largest slave dungeon in the world, the Elmira Slave Dungeon.

Minister Louis Farrakhan's wife Khadijah Farrakhan (Left) and Nana Konadu Agyeman-Rawlings – former 1st lady of Ghana with Alderman Tillman.

Phenomenal women. Tillman, in a white bowler hat and Chicago businesswoman and longtime family friend, Juanita Jordan catch up on old times at the awards reception.

Tillman receives the 'Phenomenal woman' award, presented by the Expo for Today's Black Woman at the Hyatt Regency Hotel in Chicago.

Tillman and the Rev. Johnnie Coleman, Pastor of Chicago's Christ Universal Temple Church.

The Honorable Judge Arnette Hubbard (Left), and radio executive Richard Steele, who emceed the 1st Roots Festival on 47th and King, with Tillman at a local event.

Mrs. Johnnie Carr and Alderman Tillman receives awards in Montgomery, Alabama during the Unsung Heroes Banquet.

Tillman and blues and gospel artist Otis Clay, a founding member and president of the Board of Directors of Tobacco Road, Inc., a not for profit organization who mission is to preserve and protect the rich African American culture .

Terry Bell and Lemuel Smith, co-owners of Hometown distributor, the first Black beer distributor in Chicago. Mr. Smith, a well-respected businessman and was a sponsor of the "Bring It On Home To Me' Roots Festival on 47th and King Drive.

Firms must come clean on slavery

City's insurers to be subject to requirement

BY FRAN SPIELMAN
City Hall Reporter

Chicago on Thursday became the first city in the nation to issue a "moral and ethical challenge" to companies it does business with: Come clean about insurance policies bought and sold to cover slaves or get off the government gravy train.

Two years after urging Congress to end "400 years of denial" and confront the issue of slave reparations, the City Council's Finance and Human Relations committees followed California's lead and took the volatile debate to the next level: slave insurance.

"Show us your records. Let us see what your involvement was in the era when humans were kept as cattle," said Finance Committee Chairman Edward M. Burke (14th).

Ald. Dorothy Tillman (Ord) City Council champion for slave reparations, called full disclosure of slave insurance records a prelude to racial healing in America.

"We will shine the light on this grim chapter of our history that continues to infect, poison and divide us as a nation... I don't think America can heal without doing this," she said.

Adversaries during "Council Wars," the political odd couple of Tillman and Burke is so determined to get to the bottom of America's "dirty little secret" that they're vowing to strengthen the ordinance before the Oct. 2 City Council meeting. With Mayor Da-

ley's blessing, the ordinance is expected to pass.

The version advanced Thursday is confined to city contractors. It would cancel the contracts of companies that refuse to sign sworn affidavits verifying whether their records and the archives of their "predecessor companies" contain slave policies. The names of all slaves and shareholders would be part of the mandatory disclosure, which would be folded into an annual report delivered to the City Council.

Before the final vote, the ordinance will be amended to include city depositories, firms involved in city bond deals and companies receiving development subsidies, Burke said.

That could put corporate giants such as the CSX railroad and FleetBoston Financial Corp. on the hot seat.

They are defendants in a class-action lawsuit filed in March that accuses them or their predecessor companies of profiting from slave labor. FleetBoston is the beneficiary of a trust that recently received a $27 million city subsidy to construct a 31-story office building at 540 W. Madison.

"Neither Fleet nor any of its predecessor companies ever sold insurance policies of any type. So the ordinance doesn't apply to us," said FleetBoston spokeswoman Alison Gibbs.

A founder of one of Fleet's predecessors, the Providence Bank of Rhode Island, owned ships used to transport slaves. But company officials insist there is no evidence the bank was used in the slave trade.

CSX spokesman David Hull refused to comment on the Chicago ordinance. The suit filed in Brooklyn federal court alleged that CSX

is a descendant of railroad lines that were constructed or run, in part, by slave labor.

The American Insurance Association said its 412 property casualty company members would "obey the law" but that Tillman is unlikely to find a smoking gun.

"They went through this in California. They found a few things. But I'm just not convinced there's going to be a whole lot of information people are going to find. It was a long time ago," said Sean McManamy, Midwest regional spokesman for the insurance association.

"We're going to go back and reopen insurance contracts from hundreds of years ago and try and right a social wrong? I'm not sure that's how you do it."

The California law resulted in a groundbreaking report that named 433 slaveholders who purchased policies, 614 slaves who were covered and three insurers that sold coverage.

Nearly 800 policies were issued by New York Life Insurance Co., American International Group and Aetna Life Insurance Co. For an average $11-a-year policy, a slaveholder received $500 when a slave died. Five other companies acknowledged selling slave insurance but said their records on those policies had been destroyed.

During the 1980s, Tillman and Burke were political adversaries during the "Council Wars" power struggle that saw 29 white aldermen block then-Mayor Harold Washington's every move.

The irony—along with the political metamorphosis of Burke, who is now raising a black foster child—was not lost on Tillman.

"Sometimes, when people get knowledge, they change. Looking at the facts might have changed him," Tillman said of her newfound partner.

"Harold [Washington] always said, 'Politics ain't beanbag,' and,

'No permanent enemies. No permanent friends. [Only] permanent interests.'"

Two years ago, Chicago joined the debate over slave reparations after a cathartic and emotional daylong hearing before a packed City Council chamber.

Thursday's crowd was much smaller. They heard testimony devoid of emotion, provided by academics.

Roosevelt University history Professor Christopher Reed noted that there was slavery in southern Illinois but never in Chicago. In fact, people would run away to Chicago to experience freedom.

"It was called the sinkhole of abolition because whites would join blacks and fight slave catchers from the South on the streets of Chicago," Reed said.

"To the credit of Chicago then and now, Chicago will have a long-running record of being on the right side of history."

"Sometimes, when people get knowledge, they change. Looking at the facts might have changed him."

—Ald. Dorothy Tillman (above), on her alliance with Ald. Edward Burke (right) on the city's proposed slave-era insurance ordinance

Ald. Dorothy Tillman and Christopher Reed, professor of History at Roosevelt Univeristy, discuss an ordinance demanding firms doing business with the city to disclose any benefits from past slave trade Thursday during a joint Finance and Human Relations hearing held in the City Council chambers.

Tillman poses with the parents of Daniel Hale William School, which was slated to close by CPS, until Tillman, a strong proponent for education, help to organize the parents to keep the school open, located in the Chicago Public Housing Dearborn Homes.

Angel Perez and Todd Banks of ComEd with Tillman at a reception held in her honor.

Tillman (Center in Red hat) joins delegation of 3rd Ward supporters at the monument commemorating the Montgomery Bus Boycott, during the 40th Anniversary celebration, held in Montgomery, Alabama. L-R: Paulette Alonzi; Virgie Daniels, Tillman, Lovie Copeland, Michele Driver and Helen Jones.

Tillman speaks at The 40th Anniversary of the Montgomery Bus Boycott that emphasizes on the significant role of the women and children who attended Mass Meetings and played a pivotal role in the Selma to Montgomery March. Tillman is honored for her consistent fight for the advancement of the Black community. Seated (L-R)the late Rosa Parks, the late Coretta Scott King, and Doris Crenshaw.

Leslie Jackson, formerly of Com Ed, and Alderman Tillman enjoying a moment at a reception.

Rite-way Construction owner Larry Huggins (Left) and businessman Glenn Hairston (Right) present Tillman with an award for her 70/30 construction revitalization plan to promote Black businesses.

The Honorable Bobby Rush, U.S. Congressman of the 1st District of Illinois (Right) and Blues legend the late Tyrone Davis take a moment to "Turn Backs the Hands of Time" with Alderman Dorothy Tillman.

Rev. Marshall, former Assistant Pastor of Tabernacle Missionary Baptist Church and TRI Board member Terry Bell.

Dorothy Tillman has maintained a long and close relationship with the King family, since her days as the "Movement Baby", and member of SCLC's advance team with Rev. Dr. Martin Luther King, Jr. In the photo on the left, she confers with Rev. Bernice King, a keynote speaker during the King birthday celebration in Chicago. In the center photo, she works with the late Coretta Scott King, at the 40th anniversary of the Montgomery Bus Boycott and in the photo on the right, she welcomes Dexter King during his book signing for "Growing Up King" at the Spoken Word Café in Chicago.

Tillman is a vision in gold as she stands in support of U.S. Representative John Conyers (2nd from Left) as he receives the NAACP's highest honor, the Springarn Medal during the summer of 2007. Joining Conyers and Tillman are Detroit Councilwoman Joann Watson,(Left), who sponsored and passed the Slave Era Disclosure Bill in Detroit, along with Prof. Charles Ogletree (Right), During his speech Conyers acknowledges Alderman Tillman by saying "The Chicago Reparations Bill that she sponsored and passed, advanced the reparations struggle. She is the greatest alderman in the whole world."

The Honorable Owuraku Amofa, Minister of Parliament and Deputy Minister of Tourism in Ghana, was the special guest of Alderman Tillman and Professor James Small, PhD., at the DuSable Museum of African American History in Chicago, to promote tourism, PANAFEST, and Emancipation Day in Ghana. He was on a 17-city tour of the United States.

PENSACOLA
News Journal

"This is a very special day in Pensacola
and in American history."
— Martin Luther King III, speaking at new street name dedication
held the same day as his father's March on Washington in '63

Tony Giberson/News Journal
John Johnson puts the new sign in place.

Street crowns King legacy

Joseph Brown III/News Journal
Martin Luther King III waves to supporters along the march route on Alcaniz Street on Saturday. Part of Alcaniz was renamed for slain civil rights leader Martin Luther King Jr. E. Randel Osborn, left, is a fellow Southern Christian Leadership Conference leader.

Tilman

"A lot of streets have been named
after Dr. Martin Luther King Jr., but
it's not common for the family or the
Southern Christian Leadership Conference to be there for the unveiling."
— Dorothy Tilman, longtime friend of King family

The front page story in the Pensacola, Florida News Journal (Left) shows Martin King, III in attendance at a street naming ceremony in honor of his father, Dr. Martin Luther King, Jr., spearheaded by Tillman in her hometown. In the top right photo, Tillman and Martin King, III address the crowd during the presentation and in the photo, below, right, Tillman, Martin King, III and a senior resident pose for the cameras following the festivities.

The crowning glory of accomplishment is evident in the striking style of her regal black chapeaux, trimmed in pearls and sequins. Tillman meets with the Honorable Cheikh Mamadou Diob, the former Mayor of Dakar, Senegal, West Africa, now Mayor of Dakar Yoff.

Alderman Tillman is escorted by Cheikh Balla Samb, at the Dakar, Senegal Governmental building where all major offices and departments are located.

Tillman and Hillary Rodham Clinton confer during a reception for the 1st Lady in Chicago.

Tillman reads to a group of children at Beasley Academic Center in Chicago.

Tillman and Rev. Louis Rawls, of Tabernacle Missionary Baptist Church, where her family has been members for 35 years, along with the Honorable Carol Moseley Braun, former U.S. senator from Illinois and Ambassador, and Chicago businessman W.L. Lillard.

Rev. Maceo Woods, of the historical Christian Tabernacle Church in Chicago and TRI Board of Directors with Alderman Tillman.

Mr. and Mrs. Charles Hayes of Pensacola Florida, presents a resolution to Tillman on behalf of the City of Pensacola for the support Alderman Tillman and the City of Chicago provided in the wake of the destruction of Hurricane Ivan.

Television journalist and talk show host Tony Brown of Tony Brown's Journal and Alderman Tillman discuss Black economic development after one of his lectures.

The National Reparations Convention Utilizes Legislative Initiatives to Move the Reparations Movement Forward

Rep. John Conyers, (D) MI, opens the 2005 National Reparations Convention.

Ald. Tillman strategies with co-chairs and elected officials during lunch. (Prof. Ogletree, Atty. Meyers, Dr. Anderson, Prof. Smalls, Rev. Dixon)

Audience enjoys two days of workshops and lectures of from reparations advocates from across this nation

By Andrea Smith

"Never forget the price your ancestors paid for your freedom!" was the rallying war cry of Chicago Alderman Dorothy Tillman (3rd), U.S. Representative John Conyers, (D-Michigan), noted historian and Harvard law professor Dr. Charles Ogletree and the other dynamic luminaries speaking before hundreds of eager attendees packed into the grand ballroom of the beautifully restored, historic Parkway Ballroom, 4455 South King Drive, during the recent 5th Annual "National Reparations Convention", March 25-26, 2005.

Convened under the theme of 'Restitution, Resolution, Reparations' by National Reparations Convention chairman Tillman, the national co-chairs and regional and youth coordinators from regions across the United States, the awesome spiritual energy and passionate activism displayed by the committed participants during the two-day conclave elevated the reparations movement to new

Please turn to page 6

"Alderman Tillman is the Rosa Parks of the Reparations Movement, having lived the struggle all of her life, from her youth in Montgomery, Alabama and Pensacola, Florida, throughout her years as an elected official in Chicago, to her global activities today. I admire her greatly for the work she has done and continues to do, and for the lives she has positively impacted across the world," says Dr. Charles Ogletree, noted attorney and professor at the prestigious Harvard Law School. Tillman has led the fight for reparations on many fronts, introducing the nation's first ordinance passed by the City Council of Chicago. Pictured below Tillman speaks at the 2nd day hearing at the Cornerstone Baptist Church, in Jackson, where Mississippi residents testified to the atrocities lynching.

A mother that always believe that reading is the foundation for education, Tillman shares her love of reading with 3rd ward children during story hour.

The color purple is regal and represents strength and commitment – two qualities that Dorothy Tillman has in abundance. Tillman greets well wishers at the ground breaking reception for the Harold Washington Cultural Center.

After a stunning violin performance by Seniors of the 3rd Ward president Zeretta Reid's granddaughter Nhyla Reid, Tillman presents the book Without Sanctuary to her.

Ald. Dorothy Tillman receives a thank-you plaque from Tony Glenn at the unveiling of his Krystle Kleer Super-market in Grand Boulevard Shopping Center. The gro-cery store opens for business in mid-February.

New grocery store clearly a victory for community

By Nancy Ryan

Tony Glenn, a onetime resident of the Robert Taylor Homes, offered a glimpse Monday of the immense pressure he says he has been under as the 31-year-old owner of the newly constructed Krystle Kleer Supermarket.

The store, which he says is the largest black-owned grocery in the Midwest, is a major anchor for the Grand Boulevard Shopping Center at Garfield Boulevard and the Dan Ryan Expressway. The shopping center was the brainchild of the non-profit Third Ward Partnership Inc. and Matanky Realty Group. One of the requests of neighborhood leaders was

cer at the black-owned Independence Bank of Chicago told him while he was seeking financing, Glenn said. "So, you better make damn sure this is a successful supermarket, and you run it well."

The shopping center, which opened in November 1988, is one of the most ambitious commercial development projects in the area. Its success has become a top priority among leaders in the Garfield neighborhood, who want to bring in jobs, increase the tax base and show that retailers can thrive there. (According to a University of Illinois-Chicago study, the Robert Taylor Homes contains the highest concentration of poor families in the

As Alderman, Tillman led the fight for the economic revitalization of the Grand Boulevard / Bronzeville community. The opening of the Grand Boulevard Shopping Plaza, at 55th and the Dan Ryan expressway was a crowning achievement, and paved the way for additional retail and commercial businesses within the 3rd ward during her terms in office. Seen here with Tony Glenn of Krystal Kleer, a Black-owned grocery store located in the plaza. Tony Glenn was a local resident who grew up in public housing and rose to the manager's position at Jewel Food Stores before opening Krystal Kleer.

Creating a legacy for future generations. Tillman worked relentlessly to construct the Harold Washington Cultural Center, anchoring the 47th street cultural arts district named in honor of the late, great Mayor Harold Washington, Chicago's first Black Mayor. "A community must control its heritage and culture, especially one as rich and diverse as Black Culture", maintains Tillman.

Tillman stands outside the under-construction cultural and performing arts complex with her son Bemaji (Left) and actor Duane Martin.

Like a proud mother, Tillman beams with delight as the work on the Harold Washington Cultural Center moves forward.

Tillman at the cultural crossroads of Black Chicago – 47th & King Drive in the heart of the Chicago Blues District.

Tillman was the keynote speaker at the Congregational Church of Park Manor, in Chicago, where Rev. Luther Holland (Center) is pastor, for the Dr. Martin Luther King Birthday Celebration

The late Mrs. Tucker, principal of Phillips High School with Tillman who established the 1st campus park at Phillip-Mayo.

Alexander Gbayee, Consul General of Liberia confers with Alderman Tillman.

Marshall Thompson of the legendary Chi-Lites talks with Tillman at the Roots Festival reception held on her beautifully landscaped terrace.

Alderman Dorothy Tillman poses with some members of the 3rd Ward hospitality committee at the historic Parkway Ballroom in the city of Chicago. (R-L) Altisha Diggs, Mary Ann Johnson, Alderman Tillman, Dianne Philpot, Patricia Pearson, Ophelia Daughtery, and Brenda Ramsey.

Mr. Jimmy Tillman and Alderman Tillman at the Parkway Ballroom pause for a break during a performance of his band, who served as the musical director for the Roots Festival for 16 years.

Alderman Tillman stands with her long-time administrative assistant, Brenda Ramsey. "Alderman Tillman is a wonderful woman – she is truly faith in action."

Tillman flanked by Dr. Claud Andersons(L) and Bob Laws (R), renowned national talk show host, both serves as co-chair of National Reparation Convention Committee.

Alderman Tillman stands with noted and internationally known sculptor Ed Dwight, who designed Chicago's only statue honoring the late Mayor Harold Washington, and the 4 statues that stand as the gateway to the Chicago Blues District, all located at the intersection of 47th & King Drive.

TODAY'S WEATHER
Sunny; 60s

Chicago Defender

SENGSTACKE
Newspaper

Thursday, April 27, 2000

Vol. XCIV - No. 255

95 Years of Continuous Publishing - 1905-2000

45¢ Outside Chicago and suburbs

35¢

Pass reparations bill

Ald. Dorothy Tillman (3rd)

Dr. Wade Nobles

Dr. Conrad Worrill

Dr. Lerone Bennett

Photos by Walter S. Mitchell, III

Council hears experts link slavery, racism and lynchings

by Chinta Strausberg

In a historic move following more than seven hours of public testimony, the joint Committees on Finance and Human Relations Wednesday approved a reparations bill introduced by Ald. Dorothy Tillman (3rd) that seeks to repay slave descendants.

124

Alderman Tillman smiles after cutting the ribbon and touring the historic Hilliard Homes, one of the seniors and family buildings she help secure funds for the rehabilitation.

Alderman Tillman addresses a group of seniors at the Hilliard Homes public housing development in Chicago.

Tillman and grandson Jogay on her float waving to the crowd at the Bud Billikin Parade in Chicago. The award-winning float theme was "Music is the Spice of Life and Education is the Key".

Col. Eugene Scott of the Chicago Defender Charities presents Tillman with the Bud Billiken parade Best Musical Float award, joined by other winners.

Tillman is known for an impressive collection of hats, and of them all, this is one hat she feels is vitally important to the health and future of the Black economy in Chicago and throughout the U.S. – the hard hat of business and construction. A. Reception for the groundbreaking of the Grand Boulevard Plaza. Herman Petty, Tillman, Elzie Higginbottom, Lucille Dobbins, Barry Chrysler, Trudi Matanky.

Tillman talks with worker at Jonesburg manufacturing plant in the 3rd Ward.

Tillman stands proudly at the South Park Place grand opening, 70/30 in action, joined by Paula Robinson, and developers Mr. and Mrs. Harold Williams, and the South Park Place Team.

Alderman Dorothy Tillman joins Peter Siu at the groundbreaking of the Grand Imperial Hotel in the 3rd ward section of Chicago's Chinatown neighborhood.

You are never too young to understand the 70/30 development. A group of Farren Elementary School students with hard hats and shovels pose with Alderman Tillman and Commissioner Lula Ford, along with the staff in their classroom. Tillman helped to secure funding for the Ed U Care Early Childhood Center that was under construction behind Farren School.

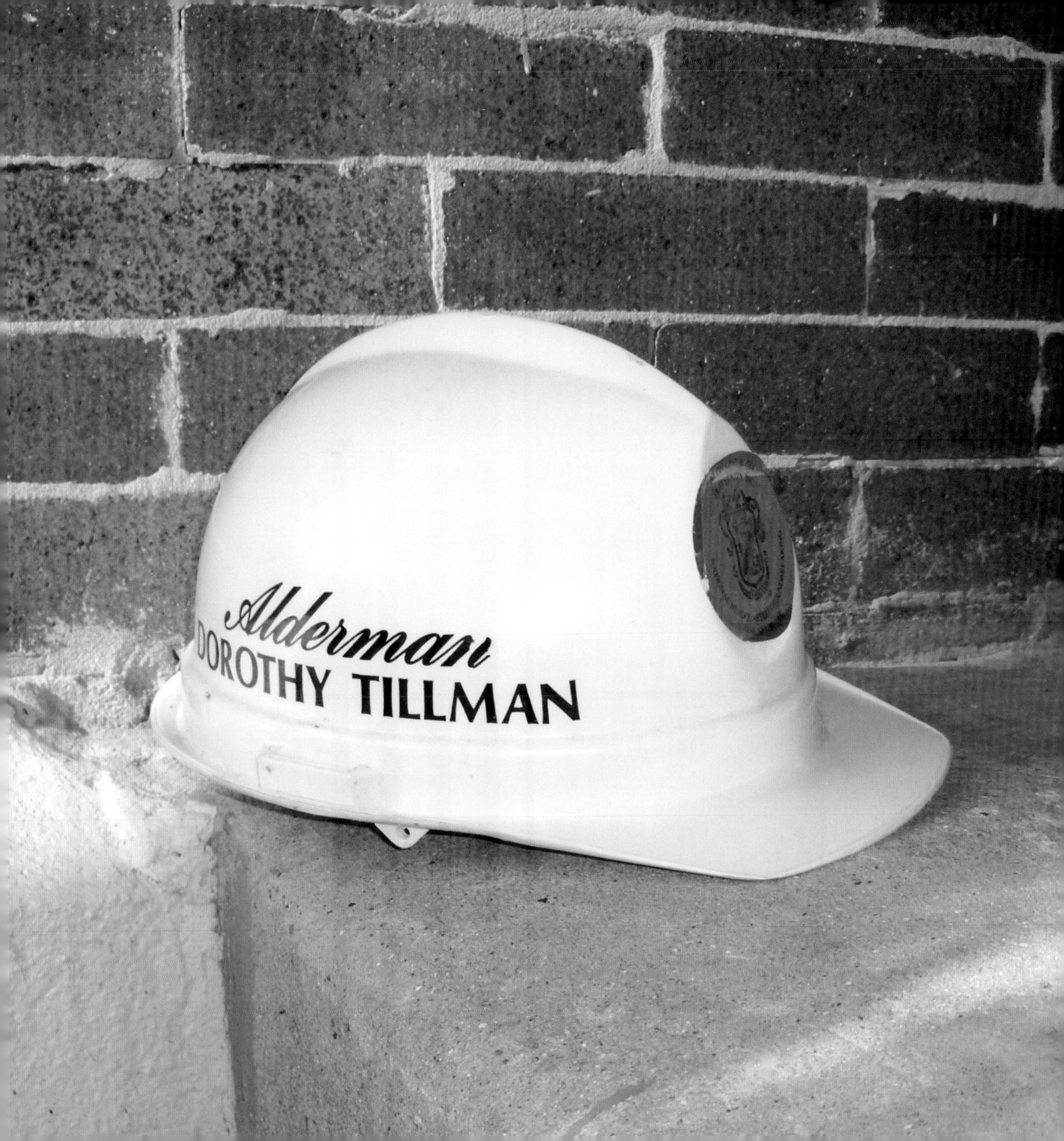
Alderman
DOROTHY TILLMAN

Talk show and television host, John Daye presents the Kizzy Awards to Alderman Tillman. Mr. Daye is the founder of the awards.

Rev. E.R. Williams, Pastor of South Park Baptist Church in Chicago and 1st Vice President of the Board of Directors of Tobacco Road, Inc. (Center) and Ms. Lavern Luster manager of Pioneer Village (L) meet with Alderman Tillman.

Noted artist Ed Dwight, Alderman Tillman and Martin King, III at the Dr. Martin Luther King, Jr. "I Have a Dream" monument dedication in Denver, Colorado.

Tillman speaks at a meeting of the West Side Chicago branch of the NAACP.

Tillman and veteran journalist, the late Vernon Jarrett.

Tillman greets former U.S. Congressman for Chicago's 2nd District, the Honorable Gus Savage (Center).

Tillman joins Rev. Father Martini Shaw and a group of children at a birthday celebration for her.

Tillman hugs her daughter, Jimalita Tillman at the grand opening celebration for the Harold Washington Cultural Center. Jimalita Tillman is the executive director of the center.

Alderman Tillman stands next to a sculpture created by artist Ed Dwight.

A host of Chicago dignitaries attended the grand opening festivities for the Harold Washington Cultural Center: L-R: Jimalita Tillman, Mayor Richard Daley, Radio personality Herb Kent, Jacky Grimshaw, artist Ed Dwight, Alderman Tillman, former Chicago Mayor Eugene Sawyer, U.S. Congressman Danny K. Davis (7th District, Illinois), Delores Woods, U.S. Congressman Bobby Rush (1st District, Illinois) Illinois State Senator Mattie Hunter and Cook County Clerk of the Circuit Court, Dorothy Brown.

Alderman Tillman has received international acclaim for her work on the issue of slavery reparations.

She was invited by Councilmen Jackson and Perkins of the New York City Council to a hearing to establish a citywide ordinance modeled on her successful Chicago slavery reparations legislation.

She meets with ordinance co-sponsors prior to the hearing, and later testifies before a committee of the New York City Council.

Chicago Tribune

Thursday, April 27, 2000

Aldermen back bid for slavery reparations

A day of emotional testimony

By Flynn McRoberts
and Monica Davey
TRIBUNE STAFF WRITERS

In the front row of a packed City Council chamber Wednesday, tears streamed down the faces of four women. An expert witness, a psychologist, was describing in gruesome detail the events of one Sunday afternoon in 1829, the afternoon that an African-American man was lynched, burned, skinned, cut and stabbed.

On the wall behind the witness were images of hundreds of years of painful history—slave-sale advertisements, notices of Ku Klux Klan meetings, photos of segregated water fountains.

Tears would fill the eyes of Ald. Carrie Austin (34th), too, as she pictured how her own relatives must have suffered. "There's not enough money in this world that would be satis-

factory," she said later, "but there should be something."

Listening to the emotional testimony of Austin and others was a crowd of hundreds, mostly African-Americans, gathered to discuss a question that has gone unanswered since the end of the Civil War: What debt, if any, does America owe for slavery, and how should it be paid?

After seven hours of testimony, two City Council committees approved a resolution urging Congress to study the question of reparations for the descendants of slaves. But many other questions remained—who should collect such payments, who should pay them, and why has this long-ignored issue seized a spotlight now.

U.S. Rep. John Conyers, the Detroit Democrat who also sponsored the bill that made a holiday of Martin Luther King Jr.'s birthday, introduced legis-

lation in 1989 that called for studying slavery reparations.

Since then, the issue has been addressed in a growing number of books, law review articles and municipal resolutions, including the latest, sponsored by Ald. Dorothy Tillman (3rd), which would make Chicago the largest city to support Conyers' effort.

The fact that black political leaders such as Tillman and Conyers are in a position to

raise the issue helps explain why it's finally getting a wider hearing. "We just have come of age," Tillman said of herself and other civil rights veterans.

Ultimately, those who want to address this controversial topic are waiting for a Democratic takeover of the House of Representatives. Conveniently, that would put Conyers in line to replace Republican Henry

SEE SLAVERY, PAGE 19

Ald. Dorothy Tillman and Ald. Edward Burke preside over the joint meeting of the City Council's Human Relations and Finance Committee on the subject of slavery reparations.

Tillman pictured with her son Bemaji Tillman (Left) and member so his band, the House of Twang.

Alderman Tillman speaks at Hartigan School.

Tillman attend the National African Summit in Washington, D.C.

Nana Konadu Agyeman-Rawlings and Alderman Tillman co host a reception as Nation of Islam Chief of Staff Leonard Muhammad looks on.

Alderman Tillman is joined by her long time friends and political allies, the Honorable Danny K. Davis, U.S. Congressman (7th District, Illinois), Left, and The Honorable U.S. Congressman Bobby Rush (1st District, Illinois).

Chicago Park District Commissioner Dr. Margaret Burroughs, acclaimed artist and social activist, as well as the founder emeritus of the DuSable Museum of African History, headquartered in Chicago, shows Alderman Tillman a replica of a U.S. postage stamp created in her honor.

Tillman stands with the first African American mayor of Selma, James Perkins, and Attorney Rose Sanders, the founder and president of the National Voting Rights Museum and Institute in Selma.

DOROTHY TILLMAN.
A RESUME OF FAITH, EXPERIENCE,
LEADERSHIP, VISION AND PASSION.

3RD WARD ALDERMAN DOROTHY TILLMAN
WWW.VOTETILLMAN.ORG

STANDING ON A SOLID FOUNDATION
DR. MARTIN LUTHER KING, JR.
MAYOR HAROLD WASHINGTON
FAITH - FAMILY - COMMUNITY
INTEGRITY - EXPERIENCE - LEADERSHIP

Tillman greets youthful 3rd Ward constituents participating in Student Government Day at the Chicago City Council.

Desiree Saunders,(far left) owner of the Afrocentric Bookstore, presented famed poet and author Nikki Giovanni (center) at a book signing in the Spoken Word Café, seated with Alderman Tillman and her daughter Jimalita,(R) who owns the café.

Alderman Tillman and Commissioner Lula Ford (Right) receive an award at Beethoven Elementary School.

Alderman Dorothy Tillman, chairman of the National Reparation Convention Committee, in a strategy meeting with her national co-chairs. Pictured: Prof. James Smalls (L) and Dr. Claud Anderson (R).

Meet the Press! Tillman is often sought out by the local Chicago and national media for her views.

The late great Mayor Harold Washington and Tillman in the Mayor's office.

Mayor Washington and Alderman Tillman share a light moment at the groundbreaking of Grand Boulevard Plaza.

A timeless shot of Mayor Washington and Alderman Tillman.

Alderman Bobby Rush and Alderman Dorothy Tillman during "Council Wars".

Tillman announces to the Chicago Media that "Chicago will give Mayor Washington a repeat victory in 1987, a prediction which turned out to be true. Mayor Washington won re-election.

Tillman autographs a poster for Democratic nominees for President – Walter Mondale and Geraldine Ferraro.

Tillman beams in one of her many beautiful hats as she attends her granddaughter's birthday party.

Tillman hosted an Annual Toy Giveaway for 3rd Ward children for 23 years, to ensure that every child had something nice for Christmas. The gift bags were filled with a play toy, educational toy, hats, gloves, socks, and a goodie bag filled with nuts and candies.

A vision in head-to-toe red, Alderman Tillman prepared to host guests at her Annual Roots Festival reception in the yard of her Bronzeville home.

Tillman join in songs with children of the 3rd ward during the holidays.

Alderman Tillman greets musical icon, author and playwright the late Oscar Brown, Jr.

Tillman is joined in her home by her former Chief-of-Staff Robin Brown, and the U.S. and London-based crew of the documentary, The Promised Land, to discuss her interview for this film project.

Tillman attends a preview reception with the other Chicago participants who were featured in the film The Great Migration, chronicling their stories moving north from the southern U.S.

Dorothy Tillman and the late Vernon Jarrett, who also appeared in the documentary, at the preview reception.

Tillman is surrounded by family and supporters during her campaign for the 7th Congressional seat from Illinois.

Tillman and Illinois Department of Human Services Director Dr. Carol Adams at the Nigerian Alliance Parade.

Alderman Tillman with Maya Angelou.

Singing duo Nicholas Ashford and Valerie Simpson with Alderman Tillman.

*The next generations of young ladies in the Tillman family
already understand and appreciate the significance of wearing their hats. They evidently heard their grandmother when
she urges mothers to teach young women to be ladies – and
to hang onto their hats. From left to right: Dorothy Darlene
Tillman, Ebun-Abeje Tillman-Massey, Dorothy Jean Tillman
II, Jumoke-Ife-Dara Tillman-Howell, and in the bassinet, the
newest Tillman lady - Harmony Addison Tillman.*

Acknowledgments

I want to first thank God for all of the love and protection that He gives me on this life's journey. From my entrance to this earthly plane, He has provided me with a loving, nurturing family, and community. My father the late James Wright, my mother Edna Mae Wright Struggs, my brothers and sisters, my maternal grandmother the late Julia Lee White, my paternal aunt Mabel Barker, my extended civil right family, Dr. Martin Luther King, Jr., and the SCLC staff and organizers.

My children, who over the years have supported me and sacrificed during this journey. Jimmy Lee, II, Ebony Tamara, Gimel Mekaba, Bemaji Amen, Jimalita Mem, and my two loving daughter-in-laws, Penny Tillman and DMetra Mays. At the publishing of this book, my eight grandchildren, Jimmy Lee, III; Jogay Ra Amen, Ebun-Abeje, Jumoke-Ife-Dara, Dorothy Darlene, Artist Joshua, Dorothy Jean II, and Harmony Addison Tillman (HATs)

There are many people who traveled with me along this journey and if I named them all the list would be endless. I would like to name a few who have particularly labored with me on this very special project.

A special thanks to my youngest daughter Jimalita Tillman for her faith and encouragement to do this book.

To my eldest daughter Ebony Tillman, who burned the midnight oil to help us meet our deadline.

To Cheikh Balla Samb for traveling with me on my first journey to the Motherland (Senegal), to experience Goree Island and the slave dungeons.

To Jason Nelson, for his unselfish time and energy as we traveled down this road.

To Andrea Smith for her long hours of assistance on this special project.

To my administrative assistant Brenda Ramsey for her unwavering work and support.

To Melody Spann-Cooper and Janie Bennett for encouraging me to do this book.

To attorney Tom Johnson who has always been there when the journey took a legal detour.

A special thanks to Ryan Gerald, Peter Siu, Helen Bailey, and Jessica Lee.

DJT Publishing has made every effort to locate the owners of all copyrighted material to obtain permission to use the selections that appear in this book. Any errors or omissions are unintentional; corrections, if necessary, will be made in future editions.

We would like to thank the following publications: Pensacola Journal, Chicago Defender, Chicago Tribune, Chicago Sun-Times, Inside the Hat, and EBONY Magazine.

Index

Adams,Carol(154) Agyeman-Rawlings,Nana Konadu(90) Agyeman-Rawlings,Nana Konadu(138) Alonzi,Paulette(98) Amofa,Owuraku (104) Anderson,Claud(124,146) Angelou,Maya(154) Ashford,Nicholas(154) Banks,Todd(96) Barker,Mable(6) Barrow,Willie Taplin(22, 74) Baudin,Jaques(22) Beasley Academic Center(108) Bedford,Ken(88) Bell,Terrence(72,94,100) Bennett,Janie(34,42) Bennett, Jr.,Lerone (54) Blagojevich,Rod(30) Bland,Bobby "Blue" (12,32) Bogan Broads(46) Boone,Elvin(44) Boutte, Sr,Al(90) Briggs,Carol(86) Broken Arrow Riding Club(18) Brown,Dorothy(76,134) Brown,Robin(76,152) Brown,Tony(110) Brown, Jr.,Oscar(150) Burroughs,Margaret(140) Burke,Edward (7) Burt,Veronica(76) Cardiss,Collins(14) Carr,Johnnie(60,94) Carter,Clarence(44) Carter,Ron(66) Chavis,Ben(60) Chrysler,Barry(128) Clark,Otis(32,80,94) Clinton,Hillary(108) Coleman,Johnnie(92) Colletta,Michael(8) Conyers,John(104) Copeland,Lovie(46,98) Cosby,Bill (66) Crenshaw,Doris(98) Daley,Richard(56,134) Daniel Hale Williams School(96) Daniels,Virgie(98) Daughtery,Ophelia(122) Davis,Tyrone (32,100) Davis,Danny(134,140) Daye,John(130) Dennis,Mildred (66) Diggs,Altisha(122) Diob,Cheikh Mamadou(108) Dixon,Qwin(14,46) Dobbins,Lucille (128) Driver,Michelle (98) DuBois,W.E.B.(50) Dunkin,Kenneth(86) DuSable High School(86) Dwight,Ed(66,124,130,134) Edmund Pettis Bridge(60) Elmira Slave Dungeon(90) Eloise Hat Shop(9) Evans,Timothy(14) Farrakhan,Louis(48) Farrakhan,Khadijah (90) Flournoy-Riser,Callie(76) Ford,Lula(128,144) Foxx,Redd(56) Fulton,Alvenia(26) Gardner,Ed(66,7) Garrett,Frank(46) Garth,William(70) Gates,Eddie Faye(80) Gbayee,Alexander(120) Giovanni,Nikki(144) Glenn,Tony(116) Goodloe,Mrs.(74) Grimshaw,Jacky(34,134) Guy,Buddy(66) Hairston,Glenn(100) Hamberlin,Emiel(86) Harold Melvin's Blue Notes(32) Harris,Louise(32) Hartigan School(138) Hayelom,Ayele(54) Hayes,Charles(14) Hayes,Mr.&Mrs. Charles(110) Height,Dorothy I.(86) Henderson,Willie(44) Henry,William(8) Higginbottom,Elzie(52, 128) Hill,Bob(44) Hilliard,Terry(30) Hilliard,I.V.(30) Hilliard,Bridgett(30) Holland,Rev. Luther(120) Holmes,Lydecia(30) Holmes, Jr.,Richard D.(30) Houlihan,James(20) House of Twang(138) Howard,Juwan(66) Hubbard,Arnette(94) Huggins,Larry(100) Hunter,Mattie(134) Hyde,Lloyd(18) Hyde,Peach(18) Ingram,Angela(84) Iwuchuku,Jennifer(68) Jackson,Millie(12,72) Jackson,Jesse L.(46) Jackson,Kenneth(46) Jackson,A Patterson(54) Jackson,Leslie(100) Jackson(136) Jarrett,Vernon(132,152) Jefferson,Matilda(46) Jeter,H.Lorraine(24) Johnson,John H.(54,7) Johnson,Tom(68) Johnson,Mary Ann(122) Jones,Adrienne(46) Jones,Lou(58,62) Jones,Helen(98) Jordan,Juanita(92) Joyner,Tom(22) Kelly,Vance(12) Kent,Herb(72,84,134) King,Coretta Scott(98,102) King,Bernice(102) King,Dexter(102)King,III,Martin(2 4,60,106) LaSalle,Denise(84) Law,Bob(124) Leatherwood,James(32) Lee,Ms.(12) Lewis,E.K.(84) Lillard,W.L.(110) Little,Ray"Tornado" (72) Luster,Laverne(130) Luv,Ramonski(72) Mandela,Nelson(90) Markowski,John(24) Marshall,Rev.(100) Martin,B.Herbert(36) Martin,Duane(118) Matanky,Trudi(128) Mbacke,Cheikh Mourtadha(54) McSween,Cirilo(84) Milton,Little(32) Moore,Eugene(52) Mosley-Braun,Carol(88,110) Muhammad,Munir(52) Muhammad,Leonard(138) Newhouse,Richard(56) Nkrumah,Kwame(50) Obama,Barack(88) Ogletree,Charles(80) Ogletree,Charles(104,112) Palmer,Lu(74) Parent Equalizers(46) Parks,Rosa(98) Pearson,Patricia(122) Perez,Angel(96) Perkins,James(140) Petty,Herman(128) Philpot,Dianne(122) Price,Ramon(78) Ramsey,Brenda(122) Rawls,Lou(58) Rawls,Rev. Louis (110) Reid,Nhyla(114) Reid,Zeretta(114) Rice,Fred(36) Richards,Don(58) Robinson,Paula(128) Rolle,Esther(56) Rozier,Daniel(56) Rush,Bobby (100,134,140,148) Samb,Cheikh Balla(108) Sampson,Al(34,86) Sanders,Rose(140) Saunders,Steve(84) Saunders,Desiree(144) Savage,Gus(132) Sawyer,Eugene(134) Scott,Eugene(126) Sengstacke Family,(68) Seniors of the Third Ward,(70) Shaw,William(78) Shaw,Rev. Fr. Martini(132) Shuldiner,Joseph(66) Shuttlesworth,Fred(60) Simpson,Valerie(154) Slaughter,Audrey Faye(12) Smalls,James(104) Smalls,James (146) Smith,Andrea(24) Smith,Margaret(58) Smith,Lemuel(94) Spann-Cooper,Melody(16) Staples,Pops(18) Steele,Richard(94) Stemberk,Frank D.(7) Stewart,Monica Faith(14) Stokes,Kenneth(40) Sui,Peter(128) Taylor,Koko(72) Thompson,Marshall(120) Tillman,Gimel(30,38,74) Tillman,Jimalita (30,38,74,134,144) Tillman,Bemaji(38,48,138,86,118) Tillman,Ebony(38,86,20) Tillman,Jimmy, II(38,48,86) Tillman,Jimmy I(48,122,6) Tillman,Jogay(126) Tillman,Dorothy Darlene(157) Tillman,Harmony Addison(157)Tillman,II, Dorothy Jean(157) Tillman-Howell,Jumoke-Ife-Dara(157) Tillman-Massey,Ebun-Abeje(157) Till-Mobley,Mamie(40) Tisdale,Charles(70)Tittle,LaDonna(444) Trotter,Donnie(24) Tucker,Mrs.(120) Vanoy,Russell(54) Vesley,John(28) Vivian,C.T.(36) Vrdolyak,Eddie "Fast"(7,8) Washington,Harold(14, 28,34,36,56,64,148,7,8) Watson,Joann(80,104) White,Olivia(42) Williams,Mr. and Mrs. Harold(128) Williams,Paul(46,52) Williams,E.R. (132) Witcher,Elsie(6) Woods,Delores(78) Woods,Maceo(110) Woods,Delores(134) Worrill,Conrad(36)Wright,Carl(72) Wyatt,Addie(74) Young,Andrew(24) Young,Wess (80)

A resolution

adopted by **The City Council** of the **City of Chicago, Illinois**

Presented by **MAYOR RICHARD M. DALEY** on **MAY 9, 2007**

Whereas, Our friend and colleague, Alderman Dorothy Tillman, is leaving the City Council after twenty-four years of selfless dedication to the people of the City of Chicago; and

WHEREAS, Born Dorothy Jean Wright to Edna and James Wright on May 12, 1947 in Montgomery, Alabama, Alderman Tillman was driven by a passion to improve the plight of African-Americans; and

WHEREAS, Nationally renowned as an advocate for reparations for slavery, Alderman Tillman was instrumental in passing the City's Slavery Era Business/Corporate Insurance Disclosure ordinance, which requires companies that do business with the City to declare any past ties with slavery; and

WHEREAS, The People of the City of Chicago owe Alderman Tillman a debt of gratitude for her selfless efforts to improve the quality of life for all of Chicago's citizens; now, therefore,

BE IT RESOLVED, That we, the Mayor and Members of the City Council of the City of Chicago, assembled this ninth day of May, 2007, do hereby express our thanks and appreciation to Alderman Dorothy Tillman for her years of distinguished service as a member of this City Council, and do hereby express to her our good wishes for her future endeavors; and

BE IT FURTHER RESOLVED, That suitable copies of this resolution be presented to Alderman Tillman as a sign of our deep respect and good wishes.

MAYOR

CITY CLERK